Stories to Nourish

the Hearts of

Our Children

Created by Laura Simms

Cover Illustration by Tatjana Krizmanic

Stories To

Nourish The

Hearts Of Our

Children

Stories To Nourish The Hearts Of Our Children

LAURA SIMMS

Contents

"Every once in awhile, we humans get it right...Such is the case with this book by Laura Simms, storyteller...A collection of 28 healing stories from around the world.   Share the stories with your own children and know that many other children will benefit from your kindness."

~CHINABERRY

INTRODUCTION

2013 Edition

History:

STORIES TO NOURISH THE HEARTS OF OUR CHILDREN was created in a hurry in October 2001 following the tragedy of September 11th in New York City. It was designed with the help of storytellers and friends throughout the world. I am particularly grateful to the many storytellers, therapists and educators who were part of the storytell listserv. The original version was printed by a generous gift from the Holland & Knight Charitable Fund. I went to places where children were waiting with their parents for news of missing relatives and families. I also went into schools that opened soon afterwards. I was hoping to offer the immediate relief of listening to tales. In the wake of such a tragic event, I learned the storytelling was too soon. Urgent, basic concerns of survival were tantamount.

When I did tell stories weeks later it was profound. I witnessed what happened when a story takes us into its embrace. It lifts us from terrors, miseries and aggressions as we listen in the moment. It was a window opened in a very dense room. Negative images were replaced by the images in a story, and the children I met were able to ask questions, share feelings and draw out their confusions having had a rich, imaginative event. I was impressed with the potency of listening that was taking place. I became more convinced than ever of the depth of engagement in meaningful stories that can be drunk in like fresh water. I still feel that the telling and listening itself is a very strong antidote. It is a worthy and beneficial experience that helps to bring our children back to their bodies, to accessing their own inherent sense of well being, and melting fixed places of fear and anger.

I went in search of tales that would offer comfort, in content and experience. It was my intention to feed the innate nature of goodness that everyone could draw on, rather than feed fear. Storytelling offers a way to process, and discuss the complexity of disturbing feelings, memories, and repeated images from that morning that changed all of our lives.

The stories have been chosen to bring children into contact with different perspectives: on death, fundamental kindness, change, friendship, and nourishing resilience. I paid attentoin to how a story moves within a listener as the impetus for inclusion. I sought stories that provided a "healing" or "caring" journey.

About Storytelling:

Traditional stories, and face-to-face storytelling, are often overlooked as the potent force that provides the ground for renewal, release from overwhelming misery and hopelessness. The intention has been to engender immediate relief from stress, fear, deep grief and intolerance, and the longterm benefit of exposure to significant conversations. Children remember events from a story readily.

Stories To Nourish provides an experience of meaningful engagement. The lived stories invite open-hearted discussion between children and adults about impermanence, sudden change, compassion and resilience. A great deal of anxiety is perpetuated in our children by their not being gently exposed to the the truth of suffering and death. They then lack the internal capacity to find calm and resilience when confronted with unforeseen events. The very fact of including tales from different cultures, particularly Islamic cultures, was part of the nourishment of the book. Today, more than ten years later, the stories are still needed. We are living in a time of increased insecurity and violence. Stories, like joy, never diminish in importance.

For most people in the world, the attacks on the World Trade Center were more than shocking. An assumed security and safety in Manhattan was shaken. Fear, and blame abounded. However, what was most outstanding to me was the experience of tremendous compassion and basic human dignity that I felt on the streets. The kindness between strangers was reminiscent of life in a small village. Storekeepers gave away food and water. People gathered in groups and offered support for each other. There was often a palpable stillness that emitted friendliness for days afterwards. As a storyteller, I wanted to see that tender quality of shared goodness, perpetuated.

To protect the privacy and/or differences that children know – from their families, religions, or ethnic backgrounds – the traditional tales are helpful. They let us imagine events without bringing up biases or forbidden ideas. Heard in small groups they become shared events. that can be talked about without triggering learned opinions. Differences can become interesting rather than conflict inducing. These tales are indirect enough (and immediate enough) to protect children from becoming overwhelmed by inner anxiety while allowing them to feel and control deep emotional response in the template of active listening.

Of course, the process of meaningful engagement depends on how one hears the stories , which depends on how they are told. Each time a story is heard, a child becomes the events and characters, even the landscape of the story,through a unique imaginative response. The stories are neither explanations or lessons, They are lived events. Therein lies their power. Stories spoken from the heart have the magic to manifest in each child as visceral imagined dramas. It is more potent than more passive media or memorized narratives or anecdotes recited by rote.

The presence of an available and aware teller of tales increases the benefit of effect. I suggest that adults, who are planning to use the stories, read the guidelines at the end of the book for suggestions about how to learn to tell a story by heart: to know the tale more than the words. To be in contact with oneself and with one's listeners renders a story a dynamic unfolding. The timing and the rhythm includes the audience. Such knowledge of attentive expression is a great example for children to find satisfaction in authentic communication and listening.

I also suggest not ending a story with a moral, a warning or a lesson. Let feelings, reactions and "lived" events of the stories "marinate." The experience is the most powerful effect. Using the complexity and multi-leveled sensory event at the service of a single opinion or lesson limits the effect of a story. Emphasis on being right separates and harms. Stories generated to have a single meaning or moral are the pillars that support genocides, wars, bullyism and intolerance. The moral at the end insinuates that the listener has not had the intelligence to garner and explore the causes and consequences of something they have moved through. The lesson becomes more about having a theory or a single perspective. That single idea is pale beside the strength of a rich lived occurrence. Imagining a story encourages the capacity to see diverse perspectives and remain curious about others.

Conversations about stories, drawings and retellings allow the associations brought up from a story to guide children safely toward making friends with their individual strong feelings. Hearing other children's responses opens a world of reliance on listening rather than jumping to conclusions or thinking one's own version is the only one. To become part of a healing community with shared sufferings is a source of joy. The way a congregation sings a sad ballad and grieving together finds uplifted solace, even joy. This reciprocity and expanded visioning is precious and rare.

As children imagine, their minds become more flexible. This is the secret outcome of a well-storied person. Awareness is naturally awakened in the process. Because of alternative viewpoints and awareness functioning, young people can explore alternative reactions, and begin slowly to take charge of their own healing. This path is one of finding renewed hope and/ or meaning in one's life, whether or not one has been exposed to a harsh circumstance. In essence, time tested tales are about preparing children to live rather than to live by one person's concepts or ideals. The children naturally become global citizens with intuitive powers of reflection and respect flowering. Morality and integrity become intrinsic choices born of being able to imagine.

The original printing of NOURISHING was limited, but the request for the book of tales continues. Therefore, I have made a revised and expanded collection. There are more stories with notes to increase the territory of listening, cultural awareness, and enriching journeys that support our children. The need for stories that heal has increased with time. There are issues that are still raging: bullying, terrorism, gun deaths, natural disasters, and increasing dependence on digital forms of communication. There is less and less dependence on the alchemy of our own minds, spoken language, hearts and imaginations. The stories offer a small key. The door each tale opens is vast.

ABOUT THE TITLE:

NOURISHING: The Bushmen of the Kalahari Desert in South Africa, one of the oldest surviving tribes in the world today, have a saying. *There are two kinds of hunger: The hunger of the belly and the hunger of the spirit. Of the two, the hunger of the spirit is greater.* Reading this made an impression on me. It is true that physical hunger is awful. But the hunger of the spirit disconnects us. It leads to greed and uncaring violence.

Stories that engage and open the mind feed us . They give us strength to not be drawn into single-story obsession or self preoccupation that promotes "getting" only for oneself. Stories feed us a meal of connection. They generate a natural understanding of the interdependence of all things. It melts our fixed ideas and engenders natural compassion. This is a relief from hatred or intolerance. When we stifle imagination, we lose access to natural flexibility of mind. One of our tasks at present is to offer our children a feast of wonder. It is an active imagination that can visualize transforming situations that appear hopeless or fixed into victories. The strengthening of sharing begins with imagination in a culture of selfishness.

THE HEART is considered by all spiritual and tribal traditions to be the place of intelligence. It is from the heart that we generate genuine communication. When our hearts are engaged, we listen to others, and feel kindness towards ourselves.

I was very moved when the Dalai Lama pointed out in a Peace Summit in Monterey, Mexico that he did not condone acts of terrorism, but if we want to transform violence we have to have compassion for everyone. Prisoners listening to stories were touched by stories I told. That was a beginning. Brilliant writer/ facilitator Bob Roberts wrote about how criminals and terrorists were often those who had had no opportunity or invitation to express grief and childhood abuse. Placing prisoners in council circles and allowing for grief to surface and be expressed, created a pathway out of violence.

CHILDREN are the future, the present and they are the fresh potential in all of us that can start again with renewed courage. If we and our children are not actively aware of the potency of imagination, compassion, engagement with others, the mysteries of spirit, regard for ancestors, and the natural world, we become blind to the possibility of change.

We fear the changes in our lives, rather than gain deeper faith in the nature of this world as it is. Without a sense of continuity between the many cultures of the past and our own family histories, we remain disassociated from each other and ourselves. We live in a story that is like an instant cup of coffee with make believe milk. It lacks depth of taste, time or nutrition.

The children of the world are in trouble. The extent of child labor, abuse, violence, sexual misuses, and use of our youth as fodder for wars is appalling. Strategies and solutions may provide plans to make change, but to endure and create genuine change we need our imaginations and heart. We must aim to reach into and under the root causes of what allows us to destroy the minds and hearts of children in the name of religion, wealth, or regional conflict. This collection of stories is a small offering.

We need to be reminded that we are not alone – in our lives, and in history. We are part of a big story that includes sudden change, impermanence, and deep emotional experiences.

To know joy, even in extreme circumstances or in the aftermath of natural disaster, is to touch back with what we inherently have within us that is untarnished by what has occurred. It is a natural homecoming, always available. As adults we often feel reluctant or guilty to feel some sense of happiness in the midst of chaos. Yet, it is that which often saves our lives and gives us the refreshment so we can return to our grief with a sense of new vigor and less trauma.

I encourage you to tell these stories, to speak about them, to read them aloud, to encourage children to draw pictures, and to share your own life tales recalled or inspired by the images and events in the stories. Sharing your life and experiences, or those that you have heard, provide children with a pattern of recognizing that tragedies take place and we can with time find joy in our lives.

A story never grows old. Each time it is heard or retold it is as fresh as rain. For some children, the security of hearing the same story with the same outcome over and over allows them a growing access to innate internal peace. It sets the ground for uncovering a constant bridge to abiding calm within their hearts.

-Laura Simms

1

IN THE BEGINNING

Adapted from A Cherokee Tale

Sent by Storyteller Gayle Ross

This is what the elders told me when I was a child. In the beginning, everything was water. There was nothing but a great ocean. Then Water Beetle dove to the bottom of the sea and brought up a handful of mud, which grew to become this land.

Buzzard came down from the world above and flew across this world. Making wind with his wings, he dried the earth, carving the valleys and shaping the mountains.

Grandmother Sun began following the path through the heavens that she follows to this day and Uncle Moon smiled at night.

And all the creatures came down from the world above to make a home of this middle world.

At that time, Creator spoke to all his children, plants, and animals alike. "It is my wish that you all fast and pray for wisdom and strength. Keep watch and stay awake. This you must do for seven days and seven nights. His children promised to follow his instructions.

Throughout the first night, almost all of Creator's children remained true to their promise. When the sun rose, only the littlest people, the insects, had fallen asleep. But as day followed night and night followed day, more and more creatures succumbed to their weariness and drifted into dreams.

When the seventh night came to an end, of the animal people only the panther and the owl remained awake. Along with the wisdom and strength they had gained from their vigil, they were given the power to see in the dark and to prey on those who must sleep at night.

Among the standing people, the trees, only the cedar, the pine, the spruce, the laurel, and the holly had remained true to Creator's instructions. To these, Creator gave the gift of remaining evergreen, while their brothers and sisters shed their leaves in the fall and stand bare during the cold months of winter. It was given to them also to be the providers of strong medicines. They were given the most sacred of all powers, the power to heal.

©2001 Gayle Ross

2

WHAT IS MOST PRECIOUS

Adapted from Syria

Rewritten by Laura Simms

Once a cunning and arrogant King asked his minister three questions: "What stone is the most valuable? What sound in the world is the sweetest? And, what is the most precious substance on earth?" The King warned, "Answer these questions by morning, or I will cut off your head!"

The vizier returned home in despair. However, his clever daughter said she could answer the questions. "Tell the King the most valuable stone is a millstone because it makes wheat edible. The sweetest sound is the call to prayer. And the most precious substance is water"

The King was annoyed and not satisfied. So he set a second test for his servant. He gave the minister a golden tray on which was a gold hen with gold chicks pecking at tiny seeds made of pearl. "Tell me the worth of this tray and you can keep it. Otherwise, I will cut off your head." Again the daughter explained to her father, "Tell the King that what is more valuable than the golden tray, the hen and her chicks, or the seeds of pearl, or his own ideas, is a rain in the spring when it is needed."

The King frowned and continued his test. He had a male lamb brought into the court.

"Can you make money from this lamb, cook the lamb, and then bring it back to me alive in the morning?"

The minister trembled, but his daughter smiled. She had the lamb gelded, then sheered its wool. While she cooked the lamb's meat, the minister sold the wool at the market. In the morning, he carried the cooked morsel of meat on the golden tray, the money he made from the wool in the market, and returned the lamb alive.

The King was satisfied, but he asked one more question: "How did you answer these riddles?"

Being an honest and a humble man the minister said, "It was my daughter and not myself who answered the questions."

The King laughed out loud. "Ask your daughter one last question. Would she consider marrying a King?"

The daughter agreed but proposed her own question. "Will the King promise three things?"

The King agreed. So, the vizier brought a millstone to the palace because the King agreed that no one would go hungry. He also agreed to fill his halls with the sound of prayer so no one would be without hope. And, lastly, he vowed that in his kingdom water was never to be wasted so everyone lived happily ever after.

3

THE TALE OF THE WATER POT

Adapted from India

Rewritten by Laura Simms

There was once a man whose job was to carry two water pots balanced on either side of a pole over his shoulders from his master's house to a well. This he did every day for many years. He grew old struggling under the weight of his burden. He used the same pots his entire life. One pot remained in perfect shape. But, the other pot developed a crack and leaked water onto the earth more and more every day.

One day the ruined pot, taking pity on his master, said, "You are my faithful friend, carrying me back and forth for years, giving me a useful job. But, I do not know why you keep me now that I am old and broken. I am of no use. I am not the good friend I was when I was new. I should be thrown away."

The water bearer replied, "I would never throw you away. You are the cause of my good fortune. Over the years your usefulness has increased."

"How can that be?" inquired the pot, "I must cause you to receive less money."

The man laughed, "Have you ever noticed as we walk back to my master's house how many beautiful wild flowers grow along your side of the road? The water leaks to the earth from the crack in your side and it waters the flowers. You have made the way beautiful. And, each day I gather flowers and give them to my master to adorn his house. Your blemish is your perfection."

And so their friendship continued.

© 2012 LSimms

4

HOW NIGHT CAME INTO BEING

Adapted from A Hindu Tale Told by D.M. Kartha

Sent by Cristy West

Once upon a time only a twin brother and sister lived upon the earth. Their names were Yama and Yami and they loved each other dearly. They roamed the earth enjoying its smells and tastes, it sounds and sights, the touches of the breezes and the feel of the grass beneath their feet.

Where Yama and Yami lived, it was always day and the season was always spring. The sun never set and the moon and stars lay hidden behind its bright, golden light. Time stood still and there was neither yesterday nor tomorrow. The flowers never wilted or died. Beehives overflowed with honey and it was never dry or cold. The birds never became tired of flying, and the trees were never empty of plump, ripe fruits. In this sea of the eternal, happy moment, Yama and Yami swam peacefully like twin swans.

One time, when Yami returned from a solitary walk, she found Yama lying under a tree as if he was asleep. She whispered his name, but he did not answer. She cried out his name in a loud voice, but still there was no answer. Then she shook him gently, but he did not move. She could see no sign that he was breathing and his body felt cold and still.

Yami knew suddenly that she was alone in the world. Her brother Yama was dead. Yami's sorrow, deeper than the ocean, began to flow out of her heart and through her eyes. It emerged as tears. The river of her tears swelled and began to flood the world. Her sobbing shook the earth and sky, and her grieving heart sent forth an intense fire that started to heat everything up. The gods and goddesses of the elements became worried about the welfare of the earth and all its creatures. They were afraid that Yami's mourning would bring about the destruction of the world.

The gods took on visible forms and went to Yami as she sat immersed in her agony. They hugged her, and spoke words of comfort to her about the inevitability of death and the need to light the lamp of hope again. But Yami was too sad to listen to consolation. She kept repeating one sentence over and over; "Yama died today! Yama died today!"

The gods and goddesses left in despair. They went to a hillside and sat in silence. Then a thought occurred to them. Yami's sorrow was perpetuated not just by her love for her brother. In her life, she had known only today. There was no yesterday and no tomorrow. For the pain of Yama's death to become easier for her to bear, today must end and tomorrow must begin.

The gods and goddesses summoned their powers of creation. First they created the sunset. Then, slowly, a gentle blanket of night enveloped the world. Under the soothing, dark sky of the first night, Yami fell asleep, just as the birds and the animals did, for the first time. When she awoke, the sun was rising in a glorious dance of colors in the eastern sky.

Yami said to herself, "Ah, Yama died yesterday."

The following day, the gods and goddesses heard Yami say, "Ah, Yama died the day before yesterday."

As time went by, Yami's grief began to lessen as the merciful hands of the night dissolved the pain of Yama's death. Although she never forgot her dear brother, her pain lost its power to haunt her. Her sadness became less fiery, her tears dried up, and the danger her sorrow posed to the world began to fade away.

5

THE TALE OF MUSSA AND NAGIB

Adapted from A Persian Story

Sent by Rinah Shelef

Mussa and Nagib were best friends although they were very different. Nonetheless, they traveled across the entire world together. It happened during their journey that on one occasion Nagib saved Mussa's life. Mussa had his servants record the virtuous deed by engraving it on a stone. Later, during their travels Nagib grew angry and insulted Mussa. This time, Mussa ordered his servants to write about the event in the sand.

When the servants asked Mussa why he recorded each occurrence in these different ways, Mussa explained: "I want to remember my friend's kindness as if it has been engraved on my heart. On stone, it will not be forgotten. But I pray that any memory I have of his insulting words will vanish in the same way that the wind blows away this writing in the sand."

©2001 Rinah Shelef

6

THE HUNTER'S GAZELLE

Adapted from An Arabic Story

Sent by Chris Smith

Once there was a hunter. He lived with his young wife and son in a village near the desert. His wife spent all day taking care of the house and looking after their son.

One day, the boy said to his father, "Dad, I want to go hunting with you."

His mother said, "No, he is too young."

The hunter said, "Let him come."

The next day, the father and son went hunting. They had been tracking a gazelle for a long time, when the hunter said, "Son, wait here by this tree. Just stay here and you will be safe."

So the boy waited by the tree.

But in the few moments while the hunter was away, a giant snake slid down off a nearby tree and bit the boy. His father returned to find his son lying dead on the ground. In great sorrow, he took his son's body, wrapped it in his cloak, and carried it home.

"What have you there, husband?" asked his wife, waiting at the door of their hut.

"It's a gazelle," he answered, "but a special one. It may only be cooked in a pot that has never been used to cook a meal of mourning. Go to our neighbors and find a pot we can cook it in."

The hunter's wife went to her neighbor and asked, "Do you have a cooking pot that has never been used to cook a meal of mourning?"

"No," replied her neighbor. "Last year my husband died in a hunting accident and I have to raise my family alone. Thank goodness, I am managing with the help of my neighbors, but we used all our pots for cooking the meals after the funeral. I'm afraid I can't help you. Try over there."

The woman pointed to a nearby hut. The hunter's wife went there and asked again, "I'm looking for a pot that has never been used to cook a meal of mourning. Do you have one?"

"No," said the woman. "Thank goodness, we are all healthy now, but last year my youngest son caught fever and died. He was my favorite, and he died so young. Still, we must accept what's happened. When he died, we used our pots to cook the funeral meal, so I'm afraid I can't help you."

In this way, the hunter's wife went to every house in the village. She returned to her husband sad and tired.

"Husband! There is no such pot. All the pots in the village have been used to cook meals of mourning. All families have known death and sorrow."

The husband unfolded his cloak, revealing the body of her son.

"Today, my love, it is our turn."

7

A PORTRAIT OF PEACE

Adapted from An American Tale

Sent by Linda Spitzer

There was once a king who offered a prize to the artist who could paint the best picture of peace. Many artists tried. The king looked at all of the pictures. After much deliberation he was down to the last two. He had to choose between them.

One picture was of a calm lake. The lake was a perfect mirror for the peaceful mountains that towered around it. Overhead, fluffy white clouds floated in a blue sky. Everyone who saw this picture said that it was the perfect picture of peace.

The second picture had mountains, too. These mountains were rugged and bare. Above was an angry gray sky from which rain fell. Lightening flashed. Down the side of the mountain tumbled a foaming waterfall. This did not appear to be a peaceful place at all. But, when the king looked closely, he saw that behind the waterfall was a tiny bush growing in the rock. Inside the bush, a mother bird had built her nest. There, in the midst of the rush of angry water, sat the mother bird on her nest. She was the perfect picture of peace.

The king chose the second picture. "Because," he explained, "peace is not only in a place where there is no noise, trouble, or hard work. Peace is in the midst of things as they are, when there is calm in your heart. That is the real meaning of peace."

©2001 Linda Spitzer

8

THE GOLDEN SQUASH

Adapted from A Tale from Tibet

Rewritten by Laura Simms

Two old men lived near each other high up among the mountains in a small village. Each owned a small garden. One old man was very generous and thoughtful. He never thought about doing things that were kind, it was just his nature. The other old man was greedy. All day long he thought only about how he could become wealthy.

One day the kind old man found a little bird that had fallen out of its nest. Its wing was broken and it could not fly. The old man felt sorry for the bird and took it into his house. He fed and cared for the bird until it was healed. One morning, he opened his door and happily watched the little bird fly away.

Later that day the little bird returned carrying a single seed in his beak. The bird placed the seed in the old man's hand and flew away again. The old man said to himself, "I have received this single seed as a gift. It must be the finest seed in the world." And he planted it.

The old man watered the seed everyday. He watched as a vine grew up out of the earth. Day by day it grew taller and stronger until one day, a squash appeared on the vine. Within days the squash grew to an enormous size. When the weather turned cold and the squash was ripe, the old man tried to pull it from the earth. The squash was so heavy that he had to call five neighbors to help him pull it up and carry it into his house.

When the old man grew hungry, he decided to cut open the squash and cook its sweet fruit. But when he cut through the skin, to his great astonishment, he found that the inside was made of solid gold.

After that, the old man thanked the little bird every day and made certain that everyone in the village received some gold so they would not go hungry during the winter.

The second old man heard about the remarkable squash made of gold and came to visit his friend. Without hesitation, the kind old man told him the story about the little bird. The greedy old man went home immediately. He took a bow and arrow and waited for a bird to land in his garden. When a little bird landed, he shot an arrow at it, wounding its wing. "Poor bird," he said and took it inside to feed it and heal it.

Sure enough, one day the little bird flew away freely. The old man waited anxiously, afraid it would not return. But the bird did return with a seed in its beak. "Now I will be richer than my neighbor because I will not give my gold away," the old man thought to himself as he planted the seed.

A vine grew and a giant squash appeared just as it had happened to his friend. But when the greedy old man cut open the squash, a fierce little man leaped out and said, "I was sent by the King of the Lower Realms to give you a reward equal to your actions." The old man scratched his head, waiting for his gift. But the fierce little man chased him down the mountain.

They had not gone far when the fierce little man stopped and said, "Had you not healed that bird, I would have thrown you off the side of the mountain." Then he began to chase the greedy old man again and as far as I know they are running still.

©2001 Laura Simms

9

THE STORY OF THE WHITE SWALLOW

Adapted from A True Tale from New York City

Rewritten by Laura Simms

When I was seven years old my favorite Aunt Zelda died. Zelda was a painter. She had red hair and wore long skirts. In the 1950's my mother described her as a "bohemian." That was my mother's way of telling me that my Aunt was unusual and special. When she died, I was very sad. I took a doll, which she had given to me, and went outside into my backyard to play. I pretended the doll was my Aunt Zelda.

I covered it with leaves as if I was burying her, and made up songs to sing to her. Then, I brushed off the leaves from the doll and with the magic that play can produce; I brought the doll back to life. Over and over I buried my doll and wished her alive again. Then I began to tell her stories. Zelda always told me stories.

I was afraid that Zelda might forget how much I loved her, or I might forget the wonderful things we did together.

I remembered the time when Zelda chased me up the stairs in my house in Brooklyn because I tried on her new red lipstick without asking. It was on the table and I was curious. I took the lipstick into the bathroom, stood in front of the mirror and made my own lips red. By the time Zelda had chased me up the steps, we were both laughing. "I will give you just what you deserve," she said. Aunt Zelda covered her lips with the same lipstick and kissed me on the cheek leaving a big red mark. "You'll never forget this," she said. Recalling this incident made me smile.

Then, I told my doll about the time aunt Zelda helped me dress my dog for a birthday party. We wrapped my mother's wedding veil around his furry belly. I laughed with my Aunt then too, because the dog barked and ran around in circles until he pulled off the veil. My mother always said , "Be careful, you will grow up to be just like your aunt." That made me happy. Zelda was "creative." I wanted to be just like Zelda.

I reminded the doll of all the times my aunt had told me stories to help me go to sleep.

Once upon a time in a village in Bulgaria there was a mother who had a little girl who was very ill. The doctors told the mother that the little girl was dying. Of course, the mother was very sad. But there was a story in that village about a white swallow. It was the one white swallow in the whole world whose wings could make any illness disappear. It could also bring that which was dead back to life again. The mother set off across the world to find the one white swallow to heal her child.

She asked everyone about the bird. But no one had ever seen such a swallow. Until in one town she was told the name of a village where the swallow was said to have been seen. "My great great great grandmother, who came from that village, told this story to my grandmother who told it to my mother who told it to me." So, the mother traveled to that place.

"I think it is only a story," said the innkeeper of the village. The mother began to weep. "I want it to be true," she cried. "If I knew it was true, at least I could go home knowing that the white swallow is real." He went to the oldest people in the village and inquired. They were very wise. They assured the innkeeper that the white swallow was just a story. But they knew the power of a story and urged him to send the mother to them the very next day.

The next morning, just as the sun rose, the mother went to the house of the elders. the eldest elder said, "There is one white swallow in the world. But it only arrives here every one hundred years. It was last seen forty years ago." The mother asked, "The it is true that there is a white swallow?" "Oh, yes," they said, knowing that it was only a tale. For they understood that the mother needed the tale in order to rest.

That day the mother returned home. Her heart was clam. She sat beside her little girl and told her the story of the one white swallow. Slowly, she came to understand that her daughter was dying. The little story helped to heal her aching heart.

The day I remembered that story I didn't bury my doll. I hugged her and held her; I cried until her dolly clothes were damp with my tears. I told my dolly the wonderful story about how my Aunt Zelda had surprised me one birthday. She gave me the dolly in a large white box with a big red bow and a note that said, "Just for you, forever."

©2001 Laura Simms

10

HOW GOD CHOSE THE SITE FOR THE TEMPLE OF JERUSALEM

Adapted from a Talmudic Legend

Sent by Rinah and Leon Shelef

Four thousand years ago, two brothers lived near each other on a hill by Jerusalem. They each had their own farm, but they shared a threshing floor. Every year they would bring in the harvest and divide it equally between them. Then they would take the grain to their farms and sell it in the market place.

One of the brothers was wealthy but had no family; the other had a family but was poor. One night after the harvest had been divided into equal measures and taken to each brother's home, the wealthy brother lay awake in this bed, thinking:

"I need just enough grain to pay for my food and servants. But my poor brother, he has so many mouths to feed. He needs the money more than I do. "

He rose up out of his bed and went down to his granary. He lifted up as many sacks as he could carry and started to walk toward his brother's farm.

Just around that time, the poor brother was lying in his bed, unable to sleep:

"I have a wife and children who will take care of me and the farm if anything happens to me. But my poor brother—if something happens to him, he will have to pay to be cared for. He needs the money more than I do."

Quietly, so as not to disturb his wife and children, he rose up out of his bed and tiptoed down to his granary. He lifted up as many sacks as he could carry and walked toward his brother's farm.

The two brothers met midway between their farms, their arms laden with the sacks of grain they were carrying to each other.

The full moon shone down upon them as they dropped their bundles and ran to embrace each other.

And God looked down and smiled.

"This," he said, "is where I shall build my temple."

©2001 R. Shelef

11

THE JAR OF GOLD

Adapted from Viet Nam

Rewritten by Laura Simms

A poor farmer plowed his field everyday without complaint. He was contented and never desired to increase his fortune or change his life. One day he dug up an ordinary clay pot. When he opened it, he saw that it was filled with gold coins. He swiftly put the coins back in the pot and buried it in the earth again.

That evening he told his wife about the pot. She said, "Dig up that pot tomorrow and bring it home before someone else finds it! It must be a gift from heaven!""

The farmer quietly replied, "If it is a gift from heaven, no one will take it."

Two thieves were outside their house and overheard the conversation. Thinking they were very lucky, and the farmer was very stupid, they rushed to the field and dug up the jar. They lifted it and shook it. It was heavy. "This is our good fortune," they said as they pried it open. But inside the jar was a family of poisonous snakes. Terrified and angry, they closed the jar and threw it into the distance.

The next morning the farmer found the freshly dug hole. The pot was gone. He was neither happy or sad, but just continued his plowing as he always did. That night his wife was furious, "Only a fool would leave a pot of gold buried in the earth. It is your fault that it is gone."

The same thieves were passing by and hearing the former and his wife, remembered their anger. They decided to take revenge on the farmer. They found the closed pot and certain that the snakes were still inside and would bite the farmer, they buried it again in the same spot. This time when the farmer returned to the field, the hole was filled with dirt. He dug up the pot, opened it, but found that it was now empty. So, he buried the empty pot once again and returned to his work.

That night his wife insisted that he go to the field and dig up the pot again so she could look inside. The two thieves, listening outside the door hugged their sides so their laughter could not be heard.

The farmer said to his wife, "If it is a gift from heaven, it will arrive in our house by itself."

The thieves tiptoed away with a new plan. They dug up the pot and carried it to the farmer's house. They left it outside the door. They believed that the pot was filled with snakes and the foolish farmer and his wife would be poisoned. However, when the farmer's wife opened the door the next morning and saw the pot, and opened it, out fell gold coins. The two thieves ran away furious.

The farmer and his wife became wealthy. But they were still content. Every day the farmer went to plow his fields just as his father and grandfather had done for generations before him. And the wife, knowing full well that they had received a gift from heaven, placed the clay pot in a special place and she too went on with her life in the same way.

12

THE SQUIRREL

Adapted from the Ramayana, Indonesian Epic

Rewritten by Laura Simms

Long ago in ancient India a ten-headed monster called Ravana the Rakshasa kidnapped a king's beloved wife. The king was named Rama and his queen was named Sita. Everyone loved the king and queen because their hearts were pure. King Rama waged war on Ravana and set off to battle. The great king of monkeys, Tong Hanuman, led the army.

They traveled until they came to a vast sea that they would have to cross to reach Ravana's kingdom. King Rama attempted to calm the raging ocean by shooting his magic arrows into the waves. But the King of the Sea rose up and said, "The seas cannot be overcome by force, but only by building a strong bridge." So, King Rama ordered his monkeys to construct a stone bridge that could hold his entire invading army.

Monkey after monkey set to work carrying huge stones and enormous boulders to the seaside. Thousands of monkeys worked ceaselessly and King Rama was pleased. Then the king noticed that a small brown squirrel rushed up and down from the hills to the shore carrying little pebbles in her mouth. "What is that little creature doing?" he wondered.

The monkeys also saw the squirrel and grew angry. "Get out of our way," they screeched. "You are too small. You are not needed."

The little squirrel looked up and said, "I am helping to build the bridge to save Queen Sita." All the monkeys began to laugh. They held their sides and roared and hopped and mocked the little squirrel. "We have never heard anything so foolish in our entire lives," they said.

The squirrel answered, "I cannot carry rocks or stones. I can only lift small pebbles, but that is what I can do to help. My heart weeps for Sita and I want to be of assistance."

The monkeys moved the squirrel away, but she continued to carry small pebbles and pile them up nearby. Finally, one monkey grew so irritated that he lifted the little animal and threw her into the air. The squirrel cried out, "Rama!" The king lifted his hand and caught the squirrel safely in his palm.

It was just at that moment that the monkeys realized they needed the little pebbles to place between the larger stones to keep the bridge from falling.

King Rama said to them, "Monkeys, never despise the weak or the deeds of those that are not as strong as you. Each serves according to his strength and capacities and each is needed to make this bridge." With three fingers, King Rama drew three lines down the squirrel's back.

"What truly matters is not the strength one has, but how great one's love and devotion is." From that day forth squirrels have had three pale stripes on their rich, brown, furry backs-marks of the great Tong Rama. And that is how the strongest bridge across the sea was built.

13

THE PRINCESS AND THE CROW

Adapted from Romania

Rewritten by Laura Simms

Once upon a time there were three princesses who were sisters. They set out on a journey to see their entire kingdom. They enjoyed the beautiful cities and rich mountain villages of their country. Everywhere they went they feasted and slept on silken sheets.

However, one day they came upon a ruined palace surrounded by a wild rose garden. The three sisters each walked in a different direction to discover how they could enter the palace. A crow hopped out from behind a bush right in front of the youngest princess. His wings were torn and bleeding. He leaned to one side. The bird could not fly. The youngest princess felt sorry for the bird and said out loud, "If only I could heal your wings so you could fly again."

To her surprise, the crow spoke, "I am really a prince who has been enchanted by monsters. In the palace is a room with a golden bed. If someone could sleep in that room without making a sound no matter what they saw or felt or heard for an entire year I would be saved. I would be a prince again."

The princess agreed. When she told her sisters what she planned to do, they become angry. "You are a fool to help a bird," said one.

The other said, "A bird cannot talk and if it was to talk it would be because it was evil."

But the youngest sister did not change her mind. The two older girls went away as quickly as they could before it grew dark.

The very first night, the princess awoke. She heard the sound of the door opening. The room filled with monsters. Their mouths were almost as large as their heads and their bellies were so big she could hardly see their feet. They darted back and forth and made a terrible noise as they lit the fire in the hearth. Then they set down a huge cauldron filled with water on the flames. They hopped up and down and ran back and forth.

At first, the princess was terrified. But the monsters were so funny looking that she laughed to herself in silence. She thought about running away, but then she thought of the black crow and his torn wings and she did not move.

Toward morning, the monsters lifted her up and carried her toward the fireplace. Now she was truly frightened, but she bit her lips and made not a sound. Just as they were about to throw her in the pot, the sun rose and the monsters disappeared. Exhausted, the princess rushed back to the golden bed and fell asleep.

In the afternoon, when she awoke and went outside, the crow returned. The tips of his wings were healed. "Thank you," he said. "If you had made a single sound my sufferings would have doubled."

Each night it was the same. The monsters leaped and danced and boiled water in the cauldron. And each morning they were about to throw her in the pot, when the sun rose and they disappeared. And each day the crow's wings became stronger and stronger. At the end of a year, the crow's wings were completely healed and the monsters no longer returned.

However, the crow did not turn back into a prince and the princess asked him what else she could do to restore him to his true form. "If you work as a servant for one year, then the enchantment will be broken," said the bird.

The princess sought work as a servant. All day she cleaned and tended pigs and in the evening she spun flax. She slept in a tiny cottage with barely a blanket to keep her warm. She worked until her back ached, and her soft hands were weary.

The year passed slowly and many times she thought of returning to her sisters, wondering if what they had said was true. But still, she kept her promise.

On the very last day of the year, the princess heard the rustling of wings. The door of her house opened and in walked a noble young man. "I am the prince," he said and knelt down and kissed her hands. "Your strength and your goodness have saved me."

Together they returned to the prince's palace. It was as new as the sun when it rises in the morning and the rose bushes bloomed in every color. The rooms were filled with people, and the garden was alive with birds and beasts. Everyone bowed before the princess and thanked her for never forgetting her promise.

In time, the youngest princess married the prince. They ruled together equally on two thrones. They ruled with great kindness, and everyone, even the two older sisters, lived happily ever after.

© 2012 LSimms

14

TWO FRIENDS AND ONE HORSE

Adapted from A Bedouin Tale

Sent by Yoel Perez, and rewritten by Laura Simms

Two men, neighbors and friends, were named Nabek and Dagar. They lived near a great desert. Nabek had an incomparable horse. It was beautiful and as graceful as a deer. Dagar dreamed of having his friend's horse. Day and night, he could not stop thinking about the horse. Finally, he went to Nabek an asked him to sell it to him. Nabek said, " I would not sell this animal for all the gold in the world."

Unable to control his desire, Dagar decided to trick his friend in order to gain the horse. He disguised himself as a beggar. He covered his face, and sat by the side of a road in a large cape, where Nabek passed each day. When Nabak approached, Dagar moaned. He called out for help, pretending to be thirsty and hungry. Nabek took pity on the beggar who he thought could no longer walk. The beggar said, "Please take me to the market." Nabek put him on the horse's back in order to carry him to the marketplace.

The moment Dagar was on the horse, he sat up straight and took control of he reins. He kicked the horse and galloped away, shouting back at his neighbor, "I am Dagar. You will never get your horse back!"

Nabek did not chase after his friend. But he called after him, "Dagar, stop for a moment. I want to ask you something." Recognizing that his friend could not catch him by foot, Dagar stopped. Nabek called out, "By Allah's will, you are now the owner of my wonderful horse. But please never tell anyone how you go the horse."

"Why not?" inquired Dagar.

"If people should hear how you tricked me, they might never stop to help another beggar at the side of the road. They will be afraid. Perhaps they will leave some poor soul to die. If this story should be told, it could cause great evil in the world."

Dagar listened. He said nothing for long time. Then, he climbed down off the horse and gave it back to his neighbor. Together they returned to the tent of Nabek and made an agreement of peace. They swore to be friends forever.

© 2001 Yoel Perez

15

THE RED FISH

Adapted from Turkey

Rewritten by Laura Simms

A kind fisherman once caught a bright shining red fish. It was so lovely, he took pity on it and instead of cooking it or selling it, he decided to take the fish home as a pet. He dug a hole in the floor of his house, filled it with water, and put the fish safely within it. From that day onwards, the fisherman had very good luck.

One day, he came home early, and discovered the source of his good fortune. It was the fish. He saw it leap from the hole, shed its fish skin and turn into a beautiful young woman. She was a fish fairy and she promised to live with him.

Soon, the King, who was a greedy man, heard about the fish fairy and wanted to marry her himself. The fisherman begged the King to let him keep the fish fairy. The clever King said, "Build me a gold palace in the sea in four days and you can keep her!" When the fisherman returned home, there was a gold palace on an island in the sea. The fish fairy had called upon the fish to build it.

The King called for the fisherman again and demanded, "if you want to keep the fish fairy then make me a crystal bridge that stretches from the shore to the palace in two days!" Again, when the fisherman returned home, the crystal bridge had been built.

The King grew angry. "If you and your fish fairy are so clever then bring me an egg with a flying donkey inside by tomorrow morning.

When the fisherman told the fish fairy, she gave him an ordinary egg and told him to throw it into the sea. He did and a huge white egg flew out of the waves into his arms. He took it to the King. Out jumped a flying donkey. It leapt onto the King's back and rode him around the palace screeching, "Hee-haw, hee-haw hee-haw!" The King screamed, "Get this donkey off my back!"

Then the King threatened the fisherman, "if you do not bring me a one-hour-old baby that is wiser than the wisest person in the world in two hours, I will cut off your head and take the fish fairy."

Hardly was the fisherman back in the door of his house, when the fish fairy said, "my sister has just given birth to a baby. Go to the sea and call for him." The fisherman went to the sea where the waves churned and up rose a one-minute-old baby. The baby stamped its little feet on the ground and demanded to be taken to the King"

Once in the palace, the baby jumped on the King's knees and smacked the King again and again saying, "How dare you have a baby taken away from its mother before it is two minutes old. And how dare you ask for impossible and greedy things." The baby smacked the king again and again saying, "I am wiser than the wisest person and I know you are a fool." Finally, the King begged the fisherman to keep the fish fairy.

So the baby returned to the sea and the fisherman married the fish fairy and they lived happily ever after.

16

RAVEN AND WHALE

Adapted from An Inuit (Eskimo) Story

Rewritten by Laura Simms

In the very beginning of time, the Inuit people say, Raven made the world. Raven was both a god and a bird with a man inside. After Raven created everything, he decided to remain on the earth. He loved the people and the animals and he was curious about them all. Even though he had made the world, he did not know everything there was to know

Raven liked to paddle his kayak out into the sea. One day he saw a large whale. He said, "I wonder what it looks like inside the belly of a whale."

Raven waited until the whale yawned. When its mouth was wide open, he rowed right in. He tied his kayak to one of the whale's teeth and started walking deeper inside the whale's body. The mouth of the whale closed behind him and it grew dark. Raven heard a sound like a drum or distant thunder. He walked until he came to the belly of the whale, which was like a great cathedral.

The white bones of the whale's ribs rose up around him like ivory pillars.

In the center of the whale's belly, Raven saw a beautiful girl dancing. She had strings attached to her feet and hands stretching to the heart of the whale. Raven thought, 'she is so beautiful. I would like to take her out of this whale and marry her.'

So he said to her, "I am Raven. I made the world. Will you come with me into the world and be my wife?"

The maiden replied, "Raven, I cannot leave the whale. I am the heart and the soul of the whale. But if you want to stay here and keep me company, that would make me happy."

Raven threw back his beak, revealing his human face. He tossed back his wings and sat with his hands on his knees. He watched the girl as she danced.

When she danced quickly the whale soared through the water. When she danced slowly the whale floated calmly. Soon, the girl danced so slowly that she stopped moving and her eyes closed. The Whale was still. Raven felt a cool wind blow through the spout of the whale.

He thought again of taking the girl with him into the world. He thought about it so much that he forgot what she had said.

Raven pulled his beak back down over his face and covered his arms with his wings. He grabbed the girl. He heard the strings snap as he flew with her out of the whole up into the sky.

As he flew, Raven heard the whale thrashing below in the ocean. He watched the whale's body as it was tossed by the waves onto the shore. The girl in his arms grew smaller and smaller and disappeared.

Raven realized that everything that is alive has a heart and a soul and everything in the world is born and dies. He was overcome with great sorrow. He was so sad that he landed on the sand beside the body of the whale. For weeks he cried and cried. Then Raven began to dance. He danced for weeks. Then Raven began to sing. He sang for weeks and weeks until his heart was soothed. Then he flew back up into the sky.

He promised the humans and the animals that he would always return to this world as long as we cared for one another and understood that everyone that lives and dies has a heart and a soul. Raven's tears were the first tears. His dance and his song of grief and healing were the first song and the first dance.

© 2012 LSimms

17

LEOPARD BUILDS A HOUSE

Adapted from A Fulani Tale from Sierra Leone, W. Africa

Rewritten by Laura Simms

Long ago the animals had no Chief. If there was a problem, all the animals met and decided on the best solution. Everything was shared and there was no discord. Until Leopard decided he needed a new house.

The animals agreed to help him build the house. Tortoise and Pig dug the foundation. Lion cut down trees. Tiger and Leopard carved house posts. Antelope and Hyena placed posts in the ground. Rabbit prepared the roof beams while small animals cut grass to shape walls and the birds carried sticks to make a roof Leopard grew more and more excited, "Make the wall a little wider," he called out. "That room could be bigger, " he suggested. "Why not make the whole house stronger, " he shouted. The animals were enjoying the work and built the house just as Leopard wanted it to be.

As they were finishing the work, Leopard did his part. He went out hunting to find food. The workers were hungry and waited for his return. However, as Leopard returned, with enough food for all, he stopped in his tracks. His house was more beautiful and larger than anyone else's. Leopard thought, "I must be far more important than everyone." Instead of sharing, he took all the food into his house and stored it away. "An important animal must stay stronger and better fed than less important ones," he told himself.

That night the animals met. "Leopard is foolish," one said. "Such selfishness is wrong thinking," said another. And Goat, known for his wisdom, stood up and said, "Leopard's behavior will only lead to trouble." Each animal spoke from their heart about what Leopard had done. When they were finished, Monkey spoke, "we must help Leopard come back to his senses." All agreed.

Dog was sent to Leopard's house to invite him to meet with the animals and explain himself Leopard was too proud to explain himself. So, the animals met once again. They agreed that Leopard was in danger.

"Perhaps we should have Elephant push down the house we have all built so he will remember what is important," said Squirrel.

Goat said, "Let us warn him first."

So, Dog was sent with the warning. He asked Leopard to meet with his friends. Leopard refused. Leopard was so insulted that he left his house and ran into the forest alone. "I have no need for your meetings or this house. I am more important than any of you!"

Leopard did not come to his senses. He went to live in the forest alone. That night when the animals met, they sadly agreed, "Trouble begins when someone thinks they are better than another." And that is how Trouble came into the world.

© 2012 LSimms

18

CARRYING A SACK OF GRAIN

Adapted from Serbia

Rewritten by Laura Simms

There was a king who took his daughter on a luxury ship across the Black Sea. The ship was destroyed in a storm and the found themselves washed ashore in a distant country. They had nothing but the now ragged clothing on their backs. So, the king found work. He had no skills, so he carried a sack of grain from the port to a market all day, every day, until his ability at problem solving gave him the resourcefulness to gain his own shop.

Everyone love the grain merchant's shop. It was well run, and he was always available to help solve disputes. His daughter was graceful and hospitable. She too worked with care and an open ear. In fact, the kind who had become a merchant began to feel content. He had never known the people over whom he ruled, nor enjoyed the details and challenges of caring for his own life. So, when he could afford to send a messenger to his own kingdom, and heard that his oldest son was ruling in his place, he happily remained in his new country.

The prince of that country was seeking a bride. He saw the merchant's daughter and was so impressed with the beauty of her spirit and the elegance of her actions, he told his father that he would marry no one else. Finally persuaded that his son would only wed the merchant's daughter, the king sent his vizier to ask for her hand.

The merchant asked, "What skill does the prince have other than ruling a kingdom and going to war?" The vizier said, "he is good at archery, dancing, making war, protocol, rulership, and solving disputes."

"Very good for a king," agreed the merchant. "But if he has no ordinary skills, what will he do if the kingdom should be destroyed?" The prince decided to learn an ordinary skill. He apprenticed himself to a carpet weaver for two years. He learned to make carpets and to buy and sell in the market. Then, he returned to the merchant, who agreed to marry him to his daughter.

After the wedding, the merchant asked to speak. He revealed his history and the fact that the prince had married a true princess. When asked why he insisted that the prince have a skill, he answered, "Until I lost what I had, I did not know truly how to rule myself and gain contentment. And this contentment, born of a skill, has finally taught me how to serve myself and others as a true human being."

19

THE MICE AND THE ELEPHANT

Adapted from India

Rewritten by Laura Simms

Once upon a time there was a colony of mice who lived in a forest. They feared the elephants. Whenever the elephants walked through their land with their enormous feet, many of the little creatures were harmed. One day, the Mouse King went to the King of the Elephants. He scrambled up the elephant's trunk and whispered into his ear, "If you spare our lives, we will help you in a time of need."

The elephant King was sensitive and wise. He took pity on the small animals who he had never paid attention to, and agreed. That day he ordered the elephants to be careful and never step on a single mouse.

From that day forth the elephants were attentive as they walked. They lifted their huge legs carefully, never harming their tiny friends. When they entered the land of the mice, they lifted their trunks and trumpeted a warning to their small friends, "We are walking. We are walking."

The mice answered, "We are walking. We are walking."

Both creatures lived more happily. As they became aware of one another, their eyes and ears grew sharper to what was around them, and their hearts grew more loving.

One day, elephant trappers came to the forest. They were capturing elephants for a human king's soldiers to ride into battle. Day by day more and more elephants were caught in great rope traps and bound to large trees so that they could be taken away.

The Elephant King was very sad. Then, he remembered the promise of the Mouse King. He called for his friend. The tiny King arrived and listened to the elephant's story.

Immediately, the Mouse King called all the mice together. Thousands and thousands of mice gathered from every direction, to discuss how they might help the elephants. No one had forgotten how their huge friends spared their lives. No one had forgotten how the voices of the elephants called out to them in the forest. One clever mouse suggested a plan. All the mice rejoiced.

That evening they formed into little groups. Each group gnawed the ropes of a single trap with their tiny sharp teeth. They worked all night. They never rested, and by morning all the elephants were freed. The forest exploded with the joyful sound of elephants and mice in celebration.

Frustrated, the trappers left the forest.

The Elephant King was grateful. He lifted the little Mouse King on his back and decreed, "From today onwards elephants and mice will be the best of friends." And to this day, that is the truth. The elephants and the mice are still good friends. Regardless of their differences in size, they saved each other's lives.

20

THE MONSTER THAT GUARDS THE FIELD

Adapted from Chile

Rewritten by Laura Simms

Two brothers lived not far from one another in a village in Chile. The first brother was very wealthy. He owned many horses, cows and sheep. He also owned a spirit that protected his animals. The spirit appeared at night in a black cloak, riding a black horse, wearing a broad-rimmed black hat and high heeled boots with silver spurs. The monster's weapon was his fearful appearance. No one dared steal from that farm. The second brother was poor. He had a small farm and two sons who worked all day for little profit. They asked their wealthy relative to help them, but the farmer refused.

One day the wealthy brother decided to travel to another village. He ordered his monster spirit to watch the farm that night. That same day his brother's two sons went hungry as they often did. They noticed that their uncle was gone. One brother said, "Our uncle has so many sheep. What difference would it make if we were to take two? If we had one pregnant sheep, we could soon have lambs and with the other we could feed ourselves and our family. We can always return the sheep after she gives birth. This hunger makes us too weak."

They decided to steal the sheep that night.

When the two brothers came close to their uncle's farm, they saw a tall man on an enormous black horse. The man's black rimmed hat and flowing cloak were terrifying. The man rode back and forth, his silver spurs shining, making a whistling sound from deep in his throat.

One brother panicked. He shook until he could stand no more and fled with fear at the sight of the monster. The second brother also trembled, but he stayed calm and watched.

The monster had no weapon. The monster's body seemed thin. He had no real form. He rode back and forth looking straight ahead, his eyes never looking to the right or the left. Thus the brother snuck into the corral without being seen and stole two sheep. He carried one sheep under his arm and the pregnant sheep he held carefully against his heart. He slowly and carefully made his way over the fence.

But the monster saw him and called out in a deep voice, "Who are you?" The brother stopped. He answered, "I am the nephew of your master. That almost makes us relatives."

"What are you doing?" asked the monster. "I am stealing sheep," answered the brother. "My uncle, your master, has so many sheep. My family is hungry. We cannot work for we are too weak. If you let me take these sheep, whose absence will not be noticed, I will share a well cooked meal with you. And, when my fields flourish, I will return one sheep and the cost of the other in fresh grain and corn to my uncle."

The monster's breath whistled and groaned as he thought about what the brother said. Being hungry himself, the monster replied, "I know hunger well. How can I help you?"

The brother said, "Help me carry these sheep to my house and I will leave you a meal in one hour."

The monster, who was never spoken to with kindness, lifted the sheep and carried them for the brother. The brothers made a delicious pot of soup, poured a large vat of wine, and heated up fresh bread. They left the meal outside the door for the monster. After an hour the monster returned. He swallowed the soup in one gulp. He ate the bread in one bite and drank the wine in a single swallow and happily returned to guard his master's farm.

The spirit never spoke of that evening to the wealthy farmer. The sheep that were taken were never missed and one was later returned. And the two brothers were able to feed their families and have the strength to work. Their fields flourished and they repaid their uncle a hundred times.

As the years passed, the greedy brother enjoyed the gifts of grain. He grew cheerful and kind. And the spirit used to frighten and keep others away took the shape of a gardener and often brought messages and gifts from one brother to the other. So, they all lived happily ever after.

© 2012 LSimms

21

RAVEN AND FOX

Adapted from A Chukchee Tale from Siberia

Rewritten by Laura Simms

A Raven married a Fox. When they had nothing to eat, Raven said, "I am going to find the Sea-Spirit."

His wife laughed. "How will you find him?"

"I know the sea!" Raven assured her and flew away.

Raven came to the middle of the ocean and sat down on the ice. Below the ice he saw a large house and dove down. Knowing what to do, Raven took off his coat, and entered the house. The Sea-Spirit met him with great joy.

"Who are you?" spirit inquired.

"I am Raven," he answered.

"Where is your coat?"

"I left it outside near the house."

"Bring it here!"

Raven brought the coat and the Sea-Spirit put it on.

Sea Spirit asked, "Do I look well in this coat?"

"You look magnificent! You may wear it all the time."

"It is not necessary," said the Sea-Spirit, and gave it back to Raven.

"Now tell me, what you have come for?"

"We have nothing to eat. Please give us some food!"

"All right! Go home!" responded the Spirit.

When Raven reached home his house was filled with ringed seals, spotted seals and all kinds of fish.

But Fox Woman was frightened. " Where did this all come from?"

"Do not be frightened! The Sea-Spirit gave this to us. He lives in a house under the water."

Then Fox Woman grew angry suddenly, "You asked for too little. I am going to get more!"

"But you will not act in a proper manner! Let me explain how things are done." Raven warned.

"I know well enough how to do things!"

Then Fox scampered onto the ice and saw the house of the Sea-Spirit. She took off her coat and entered.

The Sea-Spirit met her with great joy. "Who are you?"

"I am Fox-Woman."

"And where is your coat?"

"I left it outside near the house."

"Bring it here!" She brought it.

The Sea-Spirit put it on, and asked, "Do I look well in this coat?"

The Fox laughed aloud and without hesitation said, "You look ridiculous in my coat."

Sea-Spirit pushed Fox out and broke all the ice on the sea. Fox was nearly drowned as she tried to get home. She arrived at the shore utterly exhausted.

Raven scolded her, "I would have told you how to proceed. Now everything has vanished, and we have nothing to eat."

They suffered hunger worse than before.

Sadly, Raven returned to the Sea-Spirit's house again. This time the Sea-Spirit did not want to talk to him. Raven stood near the entrance, and called out, "I have come again. Please let me enter."

"What do you want?" answered The Spirit at last.

Raven spoke softly, "Sea-Spirit! I have lost everything you gave me, and we are suffering. Give us something, even if it is very small!"

The Sea-Spirit laughed aloud. "It is true you are suffering! Where is your coat?"

"It is outside, near the house."

"Bring it here!" and Raven brought it, and the Sea-Spirit put it on. "Do I look well in this coat?"

"You look beautiful in the coat. You may wear it all the time."

"I will." And the Sea Spirit took Raven's coat for himself.

Then he asked, "What do you want from me?"

"I want herds of reindeer and mountain-sheep."

"You will have them all."

Raven came home, and saw a large reindeer-herd. There were herdsmen who said, "Tell us what we are to do. You are our master."

"I am not your master. I am too poor for that."

"But the Sea-Spirit has sent us all to be instructed by you."

From that time, Raven lived without a coat. He lived with the Fox, who had been nearly drowned. They ate good meat, and became wealthy. Fox had a son and a daughter. Neither forgot what had happened. And that is the end.

22

THE SUN MAN

Adapted from Africa

Rewritten by Laura Simms

Once upon a time the sun was not in the sky. The light of the day came from a boy who was called the Sun Man. He had a ball of fire under his arm pits. When the Sun Man lifted up his arms, it was day. When he put down his arms it was night. Everyone loved the Sun Man because he brought them light and warmth. Each morning, everyone made their way to the large cave at the outskirts of the village where the Sun Man slept. They would call out to him,

♫*Sun Man, Sun Man*

Give us your light.

Sun Man, Sun Man

Chase away the night. ♫

Before long a very tall young man would appear at the entrance to the cave. He would spread his arms wide and look up at the sky. Years passed and the Sun Man always lifted his arms. But when he grew old, he began to grow tired. Sometimes he would let his arms slip down during the day. But the people would always call out, "SUN MAN. LIFT UP YOUR ARMS." And he would.

But one day the Sun Man grew so old and so tired, that he went into the cave before the morning was past, and he lay down and went back to sleep. The people called out. But the Sun Man remained asleep. No matter how much they called and sang, he did not come out of the cave. And the day grew dark and there was no light.

Finally, the grandmothers and grandfathers, the mothers and fathers, and all the uncles and aunts said to the children, "Children, you must go into the cave of the Sun Man and carry him out."

They said,

CHILDREN GO SLOWLY. CHILDREN GO CAREFULLY

LIFT UP THE SUN MAN AND BRING HIM OUTSIDE.

So, the children walked into the dark cave together. As they moved deeper and deeper into the cave they could see the Sun Man sleeping on his bed of stone. They tucked their hands under him gently and lifted him up. They carried him outside the mouth of the cave.

Then the children began to turn faster and faster as they lifted the Sun Man above their heads. Then with all of their strength they threw him into the sky. The Sun Man rose up and became a ball of fire twirling and twirling higher and higher into the sky. Unti, he turned into the Sun.

What the villagers did not hear, was the conversation between the Moon who was in the sky, and the Sun when he first arrived.

The Moon said, "What are you doing here? This is my sky."

The Sun answered, "I used to be a Man who made light for the day. But now I am here. You bring the light in the night and I made the day bright."

The moon thought and then said, "I will circle the earth and bring light in the night. And you can provide the light for the day."

This is the story of how the Sun Man became the Sun in the sky and and how the Moon and the Sun still take turns giving light by night and day.

Even today, children still sing,

♫*Sun Man, Sun Man*

Give us your light.

Sun Man, Sun Man

Chase away the night. ♫

And that is how it has been ever since.

© 2012 LSimms

23

THE YOUNG MAN AND THE RIVER

Adapted from Angola

Rewritten by Laura Simms

Long ago a poor family gave a child to an uncle in exchange for a much-needed ox. The little boy was forced to work, wore only rags, and was treated unkindly. And, when his indenture was complete, no one came for him. His family had suffered a tragedy and were all dead. The young man had no choice but to remain with the uncle.

One night he dreamed that a river spoke to him. "Tomorrow morning before everyone wakes up, go the water and choose one of three things that will appear. Remember, of the three, the basket is the most valuable." When the young man awoke he thought, "It was only a dream."

Three nights later he dreamed the same dream again, so he went to the river. First a bundle of guns floated by. He let them pass. Then, two bales of cloth came by. He let them pass. After a few minutes, a small basket appeared. The boy lifted it from the water and returned home. He hid it in the tall grass. Because he had been gone, and did not return until night, his uncle gave him twice as much to do.

Tired as he was, the boy opened the basket to look inside. It was filled with seeds, plants and roots. That night he had another dream. The river said, "Each plant cures a different disease." Night after night, the river taught him the way to cure all illnesses, sorrows and sores. The boy began to travel to different villages and worked as a doctor. He was highly respected. Soon, he earned enough money to buy his freedom. He paid three cows for his own life. He moved away from the uncle, built a house and was soon married. He became a great doctor and lived a good life. This young man, who had only misfortune, was given a gift by the river.

© 2012 LSimms

24

MONKEY BUILDS A HOUSE

Adapted from Equatorial Guinea

Rewritten by Laura Simms

Long ago the monkeys envied people because they had houses and remained dry at night in the rainy season. Hence, a group of monkeys once went from the forest to a village to learn to build houses of their own. Excited, the monkeys returned to the forest.

When the sun began to shine, the monkeys began to work. Chattering and leaping they gathered fronds to weave rooftops, piled branches and wood for walls and wove ropes to hold their houses together. But when the rains came early, they left their work and huddled in the tree branches to stay dry. "We will return to work later," they said.

All through the rainy season the monkeys spoke excitedly about their building project. The moment that the rains stopped, and the sun was shining the monkeys scurried out of the trees to gather fruit and dry their coats. The fruits were delicious and the sunshine intoxicating. So, the work was put off for weeks again. The monkeys promised every evening to begin the next day. But the rainy season began again and the houses remained unbuilt.

As soon as the sun shone the monkeys once again discussed their project and decided to only gather fruit and play in the warm sun for a few days. But each day they put off their plan and the work remained undone.

In fact, they had such a good time leaping from tree to tree and discussing their plans that they gave up building the houses and turned their project into a story. Even today they live in trees. But from time to time someone remembers the old tale and the monkeys promise that as soon as the sun shines they will begin to work. And so it was and so it is even today. When the rain falls, the monkeys huddle in the branches to keep dry, telling stories, and when the sun shines, they gather fruit and play and talk about what might have been.

© 2012 LSimms

25

THE WHITE CROCODILE

Adapted from Malaysia

Rewritten by Laura Simms

A very long time ago while two fishermen were at sea, a great storm suddenly began. The waves rose as tall as high mountains. The two men fought hard to steer their boat toward shore, but they could not fight against the fierce winds. The little boat was tossed like a twig and the fishermen were thrown into the sea.

Suddenly, a huge white crocodile swam towards them slowly. The fishermen were not afraid and grabbed a hold of the crocodile's body as the animal swam with them to the shore. "Kind crocodile" said the men, "You have saved our lives." The creature turned and sank back into the sea.

The very next day the two men, startled by what had occurred, sought the wisdom of a sage living in the forest. The wise man told them a tale, "Many years ago there was a man who lived alone in the forest without friends or family. Each day he shared whatever food he found with the animals. He even left food for the feared crocodiles. Then one day, greedy people came to buy his land. The old man did not want to sell his land, but the men tied him up, carried him to a swamp, and threw him into the water. They were sure the crocodiles would eat him. But the crocodiles did not harm the man who had fed them. Instead, the animals lifted him on their backs and carried him back to the shore safely. Having lost his land, the man said, 'I would be happier as a crocodile.' So the crocodiles pushed him back into the water and with a magic, that only they understood, turned him into a white crocodile." That was the story the two fishermen heard.

From that day forth, they left food at the shore everyday for the white crocodile. They always called out, "Friend crocodile, thank you for saving our lives." And they lived happily and safely ever after.

© 2012 LSimms

26

THE CAT WHO RUBBED HIS CHIN

Adapted from Oman

Rewritten by Laura Simms

There was once a cat resting on the dry, heated tiles of a rooftop in the sun, when a rat suddenly scampered above him on a higher part of the roof. The cat called out, "What are you doing disturbing my sleep? I could easily catch you with one swipe of my paw if I was not busy resting."

The rat responded, "You had best leave me alone, friend cat. I am much swifter than you." But at that moment, the rat tripped over a waterspout, pouring water onto the cat who detested water. Then the rat tumbled down between the cat's paws. To make matters worse the rat trembled spraying water onto the cat's whiskers. The cat growled and caught the rat in his claws. "I hate water," yowled the cat.

"Uncle cat," pleaded the rat, "I am so sorry for what has happened. It was a terrible mistake of destiny that I sprayed you with water and disturbed your peace. Before you eat me, at least let me pray and atone for what I have done. Friend, why don't you join me in prayer?"

The cat was very moved by the rat's request for prayer and agreed. The rat lifted his two little paws in prayer, and the cat lifted his paws as well, dropping the rat. The clever creature scampered away calling out, "God has forgiven me. God has forgiven me."

If you see a cat rub his face today, you know he is still remembering the smell of the rat that he almost ate and the water that splashed his whiskers.

27

THE WATER OF LIFE

Adapted from Yemen

Rewritten by Laura Simms

When the great King Solomon was very old, he was sad. He feared that when he died his wisdom and his life story would be forgotten. Then, a maiden told him that if he would drink the Waters of Life from a spring in the Garden of Eden, he could live forever.

Solomon called on the eagle, bravest of animals, to make the journey and bring him the waters of life. The eagle gladly agreed and succeeded in his journey. But just as the King was about to open the flask, his advisors warned him, "If you live forever, Oh King, you will become a wrinkled old creature. In a short time none will regard you with respect. But if you naturally die, the memory of your life story and your wisdom will never be forgotten. Thus, in the future, more and more people will benefit from what you have achieved."

The King reflected carefully on the words of his trusted advisors. He did not open the flask, but held it in his hands for a long time. Then, he called the eagle to him once again. He requested the bird to make the same journey and return the waters of life to the Garden of Eden. Tired as he was, the creature bowed with tenderness to the generous King and took hold of the flask in his withered claws and flew away.

As the eagle passed over the country of Yemen, the sun grew hotter and hotter and the bird became weaker and weaker. Tiny drops of water fell from the flask onto the earth. Each place where a drop fell a small and fragrant bush sprang up from the ground. It is said that the water of life produced the first coffee plants that woke people in the morning and satisfied their thirst in the heat. Even today, coffee is considered the water of life in Yemen.

© 2012 LSimms

28

THE LAST PEARL

Adapted from Hans Christian Anderson

Rewritten by Laura Simms

A little boy was born in a very wealthy and happy home where everyone was content. The child lay with his mother in bed. Only a heavily shaded lamp illuminated the dark room where heavy silk curtains were drawn to keep out any light from the windows. The carpets were as thick as moss. Everything in the room felt as if it was asleep. Even the nurse was asleep because this house was secure.

The guardian spirit of the baby boy stood beside the bed. A circle of small stars surrounded his head. They were the pearls from fortune's necklace. As always happens, even though we do not know about it, the fairies come at birth and give gifts to a newborn baby. The angel spirit said satisfied, "Every good gift has been brought and accepted: wealth, health, love and happiness."

However, another voice was nearby said, "No. One fairy has not brought her gift yet!" It was the child's own guardian angel. She spoke again, "She will bring it sooner or later, though years may go by before she comes. The last of the pearls are still missing."

The other fairy stamped her tiny foot, "Nothing must be missing. If what you say is true, then we must go to the mighty fairy and ask her for her gift tonight."

The guardian angel said, "Be patient. She will come. Her pearl is necessary for the necklace."

The angel demanded impatiently, "Tell me where she lives. I will go and get it."

"If you must," sighed the guardian of the child's spirit. "I will take you there although she has no permanent home and is always traveling. She visits kings in their palaces and the poorest of the poor in their hovels. No house exists in this world that has not had her enter at least once. To all she brings her gift. This little baby will also meet her. But since you think that time is too long in the distance, there is no reason to waste it."

Hand-in-hand the two spirits flew from the room to seek the Great Fairy in the place where she was to be found at that moment. They came to a large house with long corridors and empty rooms. Everything in that house was quiet. But the windows were wide open. Long white curtains moved in the slow breeze. In the middle of the bedroom was a coffin. In it lay the body of a woman, neither young nor old. Freshly picked roses covered her body and among the flowers her folded hands could be seen. Her face was noble and looked upwards, transfigured by death.

A man and many children stood beside the coffin. They were saying goodbye. They watched the father bend down and kiss his wife's hand that was now as cold and withered as a leaf.

They all wept without saying a word. The silence held a world of pain. Then, still crying, they left the room. One candle burned in the room. For a second it seemed almost to go out and then it blazed upwards and was still again.

The two angels watched as strangers then entered, closed the coffin and hammered down the lid.

The impatient angel asked, "Where have you taken me? Is this where the fairy that has the last pearl lives?"

"In this holy hour, she can be found living here," the guardian angel answered, pointing to the corner.

There sat a woman draped in a black robe on a chair where the mother used to sit. Besides her was a table covered by flowers and photos. It was Sorrow herself.

A tear dropped from her eyes and before it touched the folds of her robe, it turned into a pearl. The guardian angel reached out and caught it in her hand.

She said to the other angel, "This pearl of sorrow must also be in the necklace. It will make the other pearls shine more brightly. In it is locked a rainbow that connects the earth to heaven. In the darkness of night, do we not look up to the sky at the stars for comfort? Contemplate this pearl of Sorrow, because it contains the wings of love, which will carry us each away in the end."

ABOUT USING THE STORIES

by Laura Simms , storyteller

"A small key opens big doors" Turkish Proverb

ABOUT STORYTELLING:

Storytelling is an ancient healing method that has always served to bring people together and stimulate the use of the imagination, innate wisdom, and compassion that provides a basis for sustaining self esteem, and respect for others and community. In our world today, the way in which engaged storytelling functions is a missing link in the healing from disconnection to an ordinary and vibrant sense of being part of the world, part of history and part of the mystery of being a human being.

Stories are like small keys that provide the "oil" to open the big doors to intelilgence of the heart. The heart of our children is the place where true learning occurs, and where enduring emotional intelligence and sense of wholesomeness can be known regardless of circumstance. The experience of listening to stories (spoken by a living reader or teller) provides an internal place of strength for children to explore and transform feelings of powerlessness and fear into courage and inspiration.

The experience of listening to a tale engenders spontaneous resting of the mind. This happens naturally as young listeners drop into a very direct reception of words becoming images as they move further and further into an unfolding story.

The process of telling spontaneously arouses an imaginative, emotional and visceral visual response. Hence, they put us in contact with the unceasing and refreshing resources of goodness, love, awareness, and spirit that we each have within ourselves as a natural birthright.

Every listener creates their own imagined story as the story is being told. The images arise within each person in a unique and personal way. The event of the telling is thus, a non-didactic teacher of tolerance and compassion. The very listening produces possible alternative ways of viewing oneself and the world that can develop into multicultural gender, and religious appreciation.

The structure of a told tale stimulates creativity and the practice of making meaning. Telling tales inherently encourages recognition of differences and similarities as human beings and our connection with the natural world of which we are a part. Of course, the stories have to be well chosen and the storyteller dedicated to communicating the story without manipulating opinions or moral judgements on the tale or the listener. The process is where the teaching arises and not in the summation of what one thinks the story should mean.

SOME SUGGESTIONS ABOUT USING THE STORIES:

The stories were chosen to offer a variety of viewpoints and cultural origins. Some are more suitable for older children, some are suitable for younger children. In general, each adult who reads the stories should decide which tale they feel most drawn to in particular situations, or for particular children; or, make a practice of reading a story aloud each day or each week as a source of discussion, imaginative play of many kinds, or enjoy in a time set aside for special intimate sharing.

I suggest that if you have a group of children, or younger children, the stories be read or told by an adult. The sound of a voice is assurance that the unfolding process of the emotional world of the story is safe.

It is the telling, one person to another, that provides a practice in resting and refreshing the mind with image and feeling that increases the strength of capacity for children to feel without panic. The living reader/teller can be touched, seen, or ignored during the story. All of these responses are then seen and felt by an adult who can adjust their voice, offer the presence of solace and their own feelings, or learn a great deal about their child's needs from the experience.

These stories have no illustrations. Hearing a story is an active, participatory event that elicits visualalization moment by moment. What is most powerful and creative are the images in the mind of the listener. I encourage you to trust that the very process of keeping imaginative flexibility well exercised helps children to acknowledge and process their own states of mind as needed. The child who can not imagine, can not reach within themselves or into communication with others for alternative ways of viewing situations, or finding language and protection for overwhelming feelings or maintain the ability to listen to someone else without reaction, or apathy.

I offer these stories to be told or read to children. You can also read them to other adults who need solace, fresh insight, relief from stress and preoccupations of all sorts. Stories contain dynamic experiences. These are all short tales so that they can be easily read, digested, explored and experienced.

A HELPFUL GUIDE TO TELLING STORIES

Prepared by Laura Simms

CHOOSE A STORY:

1. It is always a good idea to choose a story that you feel comfortable with; and that you like.

2. A good story is one that creates a vivid experience for a listener. I suggest avoiding a moral at the end. A story is not an explanation. A story presents the situation and the ethics or meaning is felt/experienced through the imaginative response of the audience. Cause and effect becomes known.

3. A good story has a dilemma at the start. For example: *"There was once a girl who loved to paint, but her family was very poor."* Or *"A noble Queen ruled the country before the Chinese Empire was founded. Once, her land was attacked by an enemy chief who was furious that a woman was a ruler."*

4. A good story has a strong ending. It satisfies the dilemma. For instance, *"The girl's paintings saved the*

Kingdom." Or *"The queen stopped a flood that would have destroyed the world. Everyone knew she was a great ruler."*

LEARN THE STORY - TO TELL:

1. **READ OR REPEAT** the story out loud to your self twice to become not only the teller, but the listener.

2. **I NEVER MEMORIZE** a text from a page. I learn to retell the story as if it is remembered. I write down a basic outline of events. For me this is better than creating a script. It keeps the spoken word fresh, experiential, visualized, and spoken from the heart.

3. **VISUALIZE THE LANDSCAPE.** Draw a map of the PLACE where the events took place. It does not have to be "artistic." It can be stick figures and arrows, or a cartoon map. Getting a bird's eye view helps to have a sense of where the story occurs. That will be helpful in bringing the story to life for others. A story is more than just what happens.

4. **PRACTICE.** Tell "about " the story to a friend, or spouse, or child. Avoid memorizing words. The text is a text. A spoken word storytelling is a different kind of event. It is not about the words, but the experience and feelings. Learn to know the story that you are sharing. Ask your listeners for questions about what they did not easily follow.

5. **INFORM YOURSELF.** Find out about objects, symbols, plants, and places.

6. **EMOTIONS.** Ask yourself the question of what it must have felt like? Also, do the same for characters you don't like or consider bad. The storyteller has an eagle eye view. Everything is intrinsic to the completion of the story.

7. You can make **AN EMOTIONAL MAP.** List all the feelings that you have known or assume about the things that happen. You can also include a list of how you felt right before the moment you read the story; how you felt during the story; and how you felt afterwards.

Before the actual Telling:

1. Trust that you know the story.

2. Take a deep breath before you begin. Feel your feet on the ground. Taking a breath is always helpful and knowing that once you begin the audience will be only interested in the pictures in their mind and not in you.

3. See the room, place and especially the person or persons with whom you are about to share a story. Remember that it comes alive in the mind's eye (imagination) of the listener.

4. Help yourself and the audience settle down for listening by saying what you are about to do; to highlight it from the information you have been given. "Let me tell you a tale.."

5. If you are nervous, don't fight your discomfort. Make friends with nervousness. Acknowledge feelings of nervousness and begin anyway.

6.. Your vulnerability and directness will help your listeners feel relaxed.

7.. Don't forget that your listener is hearing this story for the first time. So don't rush or think you have to be overly dramatic. Listeners will feel and imagine and enjoy on their own.

8. Remember that as the storyteller, you have lived through the events. You know the end of the story. So keep the telling of the

tale in the past and not in the present tense. At present you are the storyteller telling them about something that happened in the past. This generates trust.

Storytelling:

1. **THE BEST TELLER IS YOURSELF** and not a character or an idea of a storyteller. This is not theater. The more natural you are, the more involved the listener.

2. **SPEAK DIRECTLY TO YOUR LISTENERS** – use your natural voice.

3. **BETWEEN YOU AND YOUR LISTENERS** an invisible and ephemeral stage is arising with images and feelings. The clarity and strength of the response depends on your staying connected to the story, and to your listeners.

4. **EVERY LISTENER HEARS AND IMAGINES** their own story as it unfolds.

5. **PACE YOUR SELF** – words travel from you mouth to the heart of the listener where image and feelings arise. Don't be afraid of pauses.

6. **LET THE STORY TOUCH YOU** but do not act out or explain the emotions you feel. Our voice and rhythm mirrors how we feel when we allow ourselves to be moved.

7. **SPEAK AS GENUINELY AND SIMPLY AS POSSIBLE.** It feels as if you are telling someone how you walked to work this morning.

8. **TELL THE STORY IN THE PAST TENSE,** because it has happened already. In that way it is a story and also it is protection to allow some distance from very strong events and feelings

9. **THE STORYTELLER IS A GUIDE** and is not an actor or an instructor. Meaning is felt more deeply. An analysis of the events, what it means to you or should mean to someone else waters down the powerful emotional and social experience of hearing the story as it unfolds.

10. **BE HONEST** about what you might not understand. Enjoy questions and answers. Let there be mysteries and suspense.

After The Story is Told:

1. When the story comes to completion, let a moment pass before you speak again. You can experience the feelings in the space between yourself and listeners. State that the story is over.

2. See your audience again.

3. Make sure there is a real ending such as "and that is what happened that day" or "the story is ended." You are releasing your listeners into their own life with the experience of the story as their own.

4. Before moving into the information mode again you might ask if people need a minute to look around at the room and each other.

MORE ABOUT THE STORIES

Sharing:

I sincerely hope that adults and children will take the time to share these tales with others. Sharing stories promotes respect between children and adults. We are letting them in on what is important about being a human being.

Listening:

Listening is a communal oasis that helps settle the mind, and calm the nerves. It draws us together in a special intimacy. It can repair the damage of disconnection that is provoked by too much involvement in computers, texting, etc. There are many important positive uses for technology, but we can not forget the greatest and most complex technology which is our own mind and imagination. Nothing replaces the full sensory intelligence and nourishment of engagement with others.

Mindfulness:

Mindfulness is becoming more mainstream. Already there is tremendous relief from slowing down and feeling into where we are in the present moment. Through ongoing listening we become more and more confident about "being present." While listening, mind and body become synchronized. Part of the delight of listening is this natural "homecoming." To have the facility to settle into one's presence, beyond one's thoughts, offers space for discernment, choice, and a sense of well being. One can feel difficult situations without falling into repeated trauma, over time. A living, genuine voice is a "cradle of loving kindness." It offers safety and fortifies trust. An angry voice or a disembodied voice that does not mean what it says, stimulates internal anxiety and confusion.

The Voice of the Storyteller:

The content of a story, when authentically spoken, can lift a child out of preoccupations and fears, into the co-creating an unfolding story with trust. Paying attention is pleasurable. These empowering capacities are grounded in the action of engrossing involvement, and born of hearing a human voice that is directly speaking to the one who is listening.

The Value of Awakened Imagination:

Imagining is visceral. It combines intuition and intelligence. It is a stronger ally than understanding. We often confuse imagination with invented fantasy. Imagination is generated from within. It helps us to be free from limiting reactions, while it stimulates practice in pliability of mind. There are few activities that promote such profound attention and personal relationship to story – with such directness, attention and enjoyment – as a story heard and imagined. Films and other media that have created images for us rob us of the act of self-motivated creativity. This allows a child to move through the journey of the story in a non-invasive way, that is deeply personal. Images imagined become a way of living through a problem or sudden event and exploring what it feels like and takes from each of us to overcome obstacles without retriggering strong or overwhelming memory or emotion. The imagined story is a valuable practice run in how we can live beyond emergencies. Often the images and characters in the more symbolic story permit a child the ability to go through the energy of a situation without placing them in a literal reenactment. What took place in one's life is often too big to be contained by a child's history or understanding. Such initial creative conversations allows a child to make bigger sense of events, and to relax with the unexplainable in their lives. Slowly, like the water that changes the shapes of stones, repeated exposure to the life-enhancing engagement, lessens the agony of repeated trauma.

How Learning is Supported:

With repeated exposure to storytelling there is an increase in literacy, compassion for self and others, and finding satisfaction in form (a story has a beginning, a middle and a conclusion that brings about a closure) and the ability to live through shared adventures with others. A steady diet of heard stories can awaken curiosity and zeal for learning because they render us excited about how incidents and history is relevant to our everyday lives. A well-told tale, spoken with care, not in a special "kiddy" voice or disembodied character, provides an example of genuine communication and its pleasures.

All of these experiences promote rich and intelligent dialogue. The experiences activated through listening to tales are mind strengtheners. Dialogue is more enduring than solutions. Quick fixes are often a means of getting rid of fear. Stories often allow us to feel the fear and have respect for the positive warnings of fear, and overcome the overwhelming aspects of fear. Through the narrative we learn to breathe strength into our lives, rather than shut down or become paralyzed by fear.

Laura Simms, storyteller, educator, and author, is the recipient of the 1999 SUNNY DAYS AWARD (Sesame Street) for her contribution to children worldwide. She is the Director of The Center for Engaged Storytelling, and performs and teaches for children and adults throughout the world. She is working on a Nonviolence and Narrative project with Aldo Civico under the sponsorship of Rutgers University, Newark. She is the recipient of many awards and grants for her work. Laura is also the author of BECOMING THE WORLD (published by Mercy Corps' Comfort for Kids Program; THE ROBE OF LOVE: a collection of Love Stories (Codhill Press) and OUR SECRET TERRITORY: The Essence of Storytelling (Sentient Books).

This booklet was created with the help of many storytellers, friends, donors and organizations. It is one of several emergency booklets, workshops and storytelling initiatives we are now creating in response to an ongoing need for dynamic living communication, the wisdom of stories, and restorative imagination.

Please go to our website to request additional information about storytelling tapes, books and performances – www.laurasimms.com. (The website for Engaged Storytelling Center is under construction at this time.)

CONCLUSION

I asked a fourth grade class in Brooklyn, NY, "What would happen if there were no stories in the world?" Everyone agreed. "It would be terrible." A girl said, "No one could explain anything." "We wouldn't have any dreams," added another. One boy raised his hand insistently. "There are some people who need a story in order to go to bed. If there were no stories they would like awake at night and wait and wait." Several children said, "Storytellers wouldn't have any jobs," which made us laugh. A boy said, "Stories make us feel better." And then another girl responded, "If there were no stories, there would be no world. Stories make the world."

~Laura Simms

Made in the USA
Middletown, DE
10 July 2015